INSECTS

BookLife
PUBLISHING

GRACE JONES

Words that look like **this** can be found in the glossary on page 24.

BookLife
PUBLISHING

©This edition was
published in 2018.
First published in 2017.
Book Life
King's Lynn
Norfolk PE30 4LS

ISBN: 978-1-78637-126-3

Written by:

Grace Jones

Edited by:

Charlie Ogden

Designed by:

Danielle Jones

A catalogue record for this book
is available from the British Library.

Contents

What Are Living Things?

All living things move and grow. Living things need air, food, water and sunlight to stay alive.

These are all living things.

Frog

Tiger

Human

4

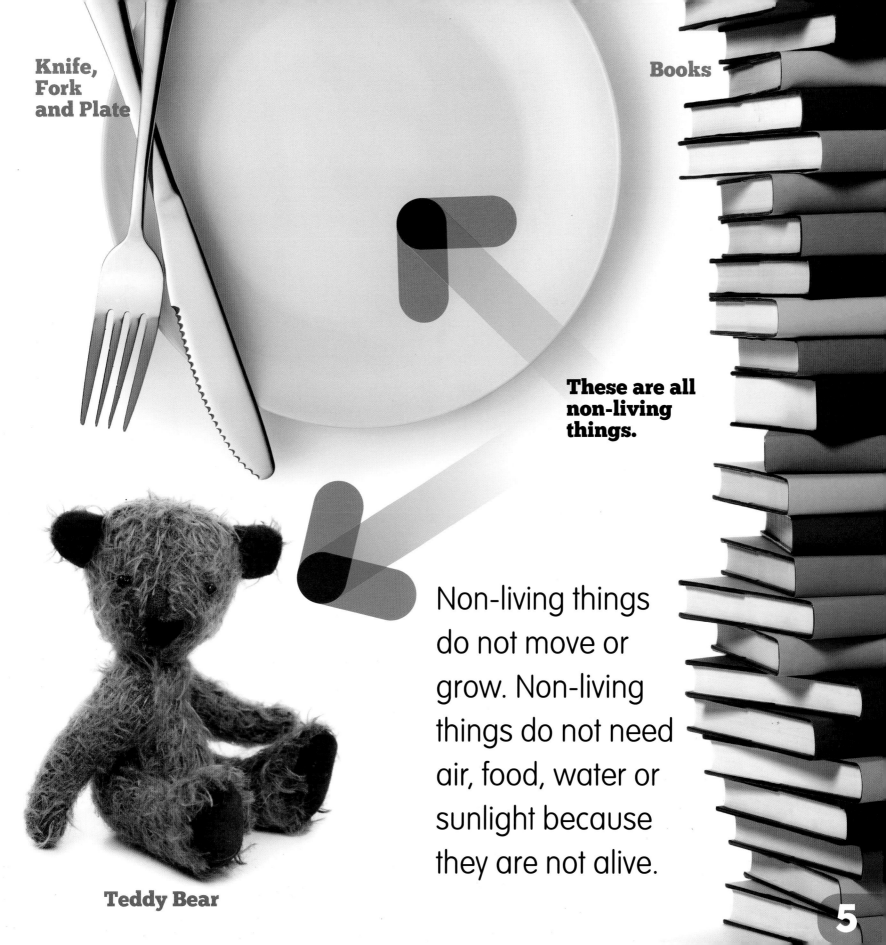

Knife, Fork and Plate

Books

These are all non-living things.

Non-living things do not move or grow. Non-living things do not need air, food, water or sunlight because they are not alive.

Teddy Bear

5

What Is an Insect?

An insect is a living thing that can live in water or on land. Insects need air, food, water and sunlight to stay alive. Butterflies, beetles and dragonflies are all types of insects.

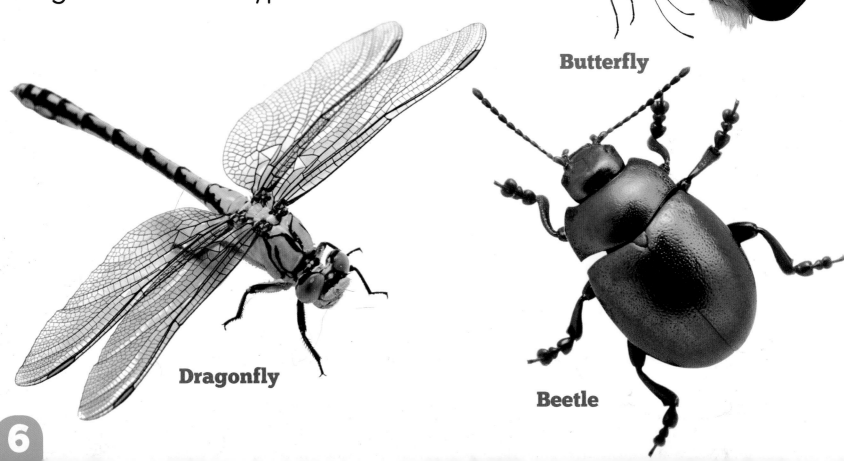

Butterfly

Dragonfly

Beetle

Insects are **invertebrates** that have three main body parts, six legs and two **antennae**. They are cold-blooded. This means that their body temperatures change when the temperature outside gets hotter or colder.

Antenna

Body Parts

Leg

Fact:
There are
over one
million
different
types of
insect.

7

Where Do They Live?

All living things live in homes called habitats. Insects live in almost every habitat around the world. Many insects live on land in forest areas, making their homes inside trees or under the ground.

A Madagascan fire millipede that was found in the rainforests of Madagascar.

Some insects, called water or aquatic insects, live in streams, swamps, ponds and lakes. These insects search for food to

This beetle eats young frogs, known as tadpoles, and even small fish.

Insect Homes

Insects live in many different habitats around the world. Insects often find their homes inside tree trunks or logs. The tree bark shelters them from the weather, protects them from other animals and can even be eaten as food.

Fact:
Bark beetles live inside the bark of trees.

Cinnabar Flat Bark Beetle

Most insects need a warm **climate** in order to stay alive. Every year, the monarch butterfly travels to a new home over 4,800 kilometres away in search of a new, warmer habitat. This is called migration.

Fact:
The monarch butterfly's migration is the longest of any insect.

What Do They Eat?

Around half of all insects are herbivores. This means that they only eat parts of plants, including leaves, seeds, nuts and wood. They use their super senses of sight, smell and touch to help them to find their food.

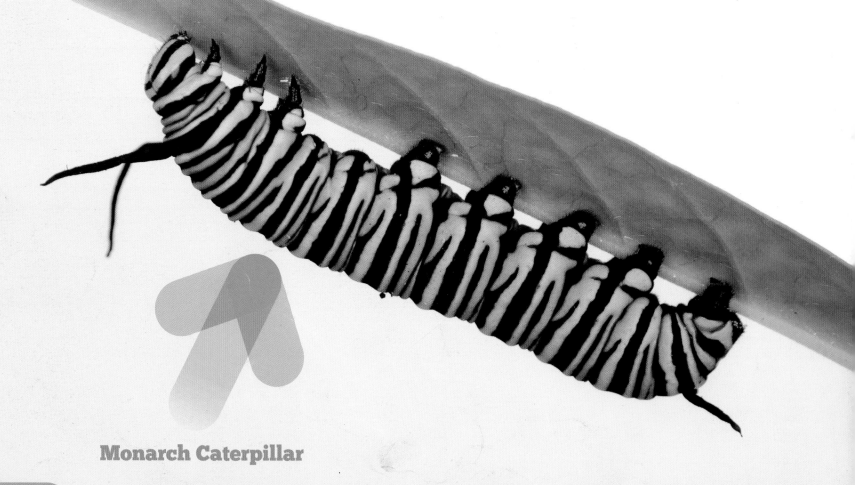

Monarch Caterpillar

Other insects, such as praying mantises, are carnivores. This means that they eat other animals, such as flies, moths, caterpillars, butterflies, frogs, mice and even other mantises.

A Praying Mantis Eating a Butterfly

How Do They Breathe?

Insects breathe through holes in their **abdomens** called spiracles. Air is taken in and moves around the rest of the insect's body through tubes.

This is the spiracle of a silkworm.

Aquatic insects have body parts that help them to breathe more easily in water. Water scorpions have breathing tubes called siphons, which allow them to take in air at the surface without ever having to leave the water.

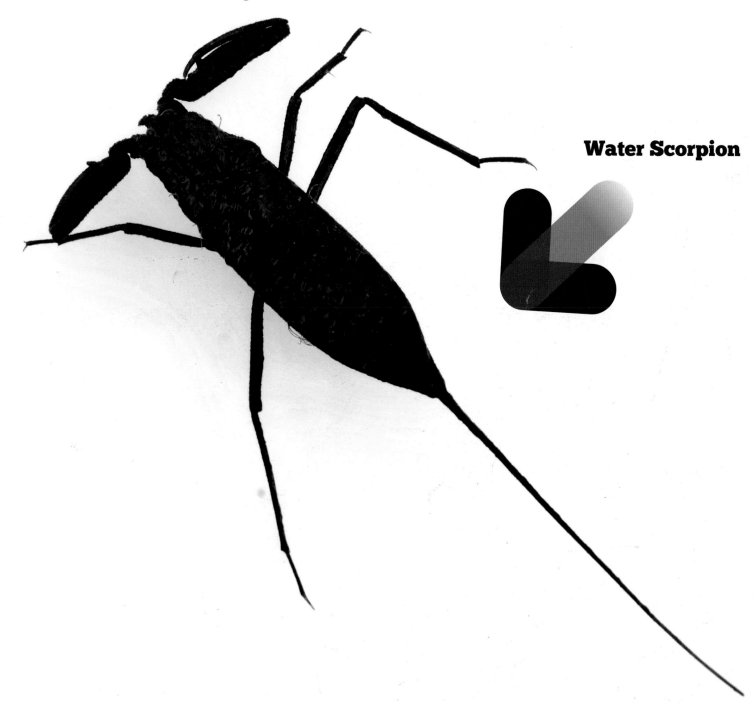

Water Scorpion

How Do They Move?

Many insects fly through the air using their two pairs of wings. **Muscles** that are attached to the wings and middle body sections of insects help them to fly. An insect's middle body section is called a thorax.

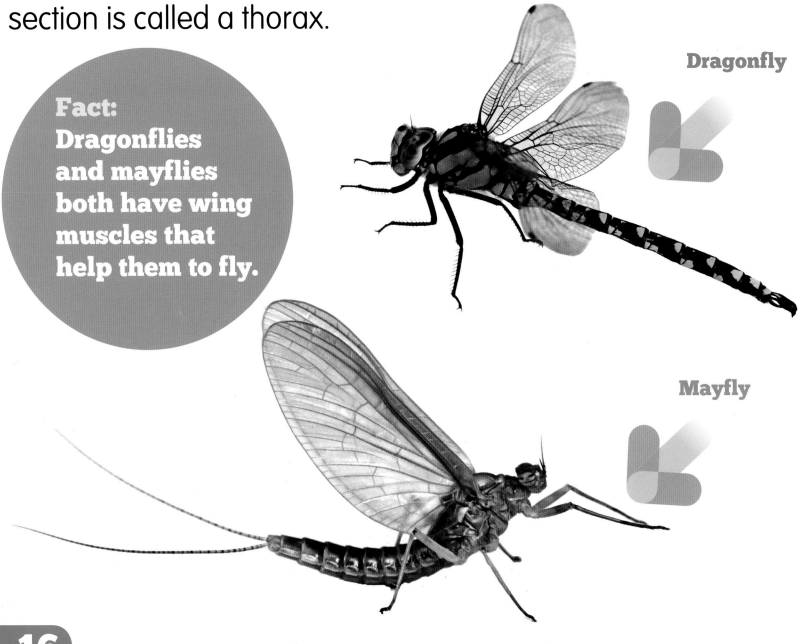

Fact:
Dragonflies and mayflies both have wing muscles that help them to fly.

Dragonfly

Mayfly

Insects that can't fly get around by walking on their six legs. Some insects, such as cockroaches, are able to climb walls and even walk across ceilings. They do this by using spikes on their legs and feet to help them to grip more easily.

Cockroach

Spikes

How Do They Grow?

Most insects start their lives as eggs. Insect mothers will usually lay their eggs in a safe place before leaving them to **hatch** on their own. Other insects, like earwigs, look after their eggs and their babies long after they hatch.

Earwig

Fact: Female ghost moths can lay up to 29,000 eggs in one day.

Chrysalis

Adult Butterfly

Caterpillar

The caterpillar comes out of its chrysalis as an adult butterfly.

After hatching, some insects still have a long way to go before they are fully grown. Caterpillars must wrap themselves inside a shell, called a chrysalis, before they can grow into adult butterflies.

19

Incredible Insects

Some insects are very colourful in order to warn other animals that they are poisonous. This helps them to avoid being eaten by predators. The jewel beetle is one of the most colourful insects in the world and it can be found in the rainforests of Southeast Asia.

Jewel Beetle

Other insects use their colourful bodies for **camouflage** instead. The walking flower mantis camouflages itself so well that it looks exactly like a flower. This allows it to catch its food more easily and avoid being seen by other predators.

Walking Flower Mantis

World Record Breakers

GIANT WETA

Fact:
Giant wetas weigh around **twice** as much as an average hamster.

Weight:
70 grams

Record:
The World's Heaviest Insect!

BULLET ANT

Record:
The World's Most Painful Sting!

Size:
3cm long

Fact:
Being stung by a bullet ant is so painful that it feels like you have been shot.

Glossary

abdomens one of the three parts of insects' bodies

antennae a pair of long, thin sensors found on the heads of insects

camouflage characteristics that allow an animal to hide itself in a habitat

climate the common weather in a certain place

hatch when a baby animal comes out of its egg

invertebrates animals that do not have backbones

muscles bundles of tissue in the bodies of animals and humans

poisonous dangerous or deadly when eaten

Index